SPIRIT 2000

Daily Meditations on Discipleship

Ma

GW00602755

P U

Allen, Texas

IMPRIMI POTEST
Bradley M. Schaeffer, S.J.

NIHIL OBSTAT
Rev. Glenn D. Gardner, J.C.D.
Censor Librorum

IMPRIMATUR
† Most Rev. Charles V. Grahmann
Bishop of Dallas

December 15, 1993

The Nihil Obstat and Imprimatur are official declarations
that the material reviewed is free of doctrinal or moral
error. No implication is contained therein that those
granting the Nihil Obstat and Imprimatur agree with the
contents, opinions, or statements expressed.

Cover Photo   COMSTOCK INC.

ACKNOWLEDGMENTS

Unless otherwise noted, all Scripture quotations are from
Today's English Version text. Copyright © American
Bible Society 1966, 1971, 1976. Used by permission.

Send all inquiries to:
Tabor Publishing
200 East Bethany Drive   Toll free 800–822–6701
Allen, Texas 75002–3804   Fax   800–688–8356

Printed in the United States of America

ISBN 0–7829–0447–5

4 5 6 7 8   99 98 97 96 95

CONTENTS

TABOR
SPIRITUALITY
RESOURCES

Vision 2000 Series

Books

Vision 2000 (A Cycle)
Mission 2000 (B Cycle)
Action 2000 (C Cycle)
Challenge 2000
Bible 2000

Booklets

Spirit 2000
Lent 2000
Cuaresma 2000
Espíritu 2000

For quantity discounts or further
information, call or write:

Tabor Publishing
200 East Bethany Drive
Allen, Texas 75002–3804
Call toll free 800–822–6701

How to Use *Spirit 2000*

This booklet involves a twofold commitment:

- to meditate daily
  on your own for ten minutes, and
- to meet weekly
  with six or eight friends
  for thirty or forty minutes.

Daily Meditation

Each daily meditation exercise contains
four parts:

- a Scripture passage,
- a story,
- an application to life, and
- a concluding thought.

Begin each daily meditation by praying the
prayer printed on the inside front cover.

The format for each meditation is also
printed on the inside front cover.

End each meditation by reciting
the Lord's Prayer slowly and reverently.
Then jot down in a small notebook
whatever struck you most
during your meditation.

Weekly Meeting

The purpose of the weekly meeting
is for *support* and *sharing*.
Meetings are 30 to 40 minutes long,
unless the group decides otherwise.
The meeting starts with a "call to prayer."

A member lights a candle.
Then three readers reverently read
the prayer printed on page 60.

The meeting proper begins
with the leader responding briefly
to these two questions:

• How faithful was I to my commitment
  to reflect daily on the Bible reading?
• Which daily meditation
  was most meaningful for me, and why?

The leader then invites each member,
in turn, to respond briefly
to the same two questions.

When all have responded,
the leader opens the floor
to anyone who wishes—

- to elaborate on his or her response
  to the second question, or
- to comment on another's response
  (not to take issue with it,
  but to affirm or clarify it).

The meeting ends
with a "call to mission": a charge
to witness to Jesus and
to his teaching in daily life.
It consists in three people praying the
prayer printed on the inside back cover.

A member extinguishes the candle
(lit at the start of the meeting)
before the final reading.

WEEK 1:
Learn of Me

WEEK 1: Learn of Me

[Jesus said to his disciples,]
"Learn from me,
because I am gentle and humble in spirit."
MATTHEW 11:29

[Jesus] never wrote a book. . . .
He never owned a home. . . .
He never traveled two hundred miles
from the place where he was born. . . .
While still a young man, the tide of
popular opinion turned against him. . . .
He was nailed to a cross. . . .
When he was dead, he was taken down
and laid in a borrowed grave. . . .
Nineteen centuries
have come and gone,
and today he is the central figure
of the human race. . . .
I am far within the mark when I say
that all the armies that ever marched . . .
have not affected
the life of man upon earth
as powerfully as this One Solitary Life.
ANONYMOUS

What attracts me most to Jesus?

When Jesus teaches me
to sing his song,
how can I keep from singing it?
ANONYMOUS

WEEK 1: Learn of Me

Day 2 _____

[Jesus said,] "Whoever believes in me
believes not only in me
but also in him who sent me.
Whoever sees me
sees also him who sent me."

JOHN 12:44-45

An old poem concerns a young woman
who is told God lives on top of a mountain
at the end of the earth.
She journeys to the mountain and
begins the long climb to the top.
At the moment she begins, God thinks,
"What can I do to show people on earth
that I love them?"
God says, "I know! I'll journey down
the mountain and live among them."
Thus, when the young woman reaches
the top of the mountain, God is not there.
She thinks, "God doesn't live here!
Maybe God doesn't even exist."
The poem's point is this:
We look for God in the wrong place.
We forget that God came down
from heaven and lives among us.

Where do I look for God?
Where else might I look for God?

God dwells wherever we let him in.
ANCIENT JEWISH SAYING

[Peter said to the crowd on Pentecost,]
"Jesus, whom you crucified, is the one
that God has made Lord and Messiah."
When the people heard this,
they were deeply troubled and said . . .
"What shall we do, brothers?"
Peter said to them,
"Each one of you must turn away
from his sins and be baptized
in the name of Jesus Christ."

ACTS 2:36-38

A missionary was showing slides
of Jesus' life to some new Christians.
When a slide of the crucifixion flashed
on the screen, someone called out,
"I'm the one who
should be on the cross, not you, Jesus."
Once we become aware
of our role in the crucifixion of Jesus,
we cannot help but be touched deeply,
as was the crowd on Pentecost.
Then the only response possible for us
is to repent and start living for Jesus.

What might I do to become more aware
of my role in Jesus' death?

Repentance . . .
is not self-loathing, but God-loving.

FULTON J. SHEEN

WEEK 1: Learn of Me

Day 4 _____

[Jesus said,]
"Whoever has seen me
has seen the Father."

JOHN 14:9

A young lady asked,
"How can we claim that Jesus possessed
a unique knowledge of God?"
It all depends upon who Jesus is.
No other major religious leader in history
ever claimed what Jesus did.
Buddha refused to be called "divine."
Muhammad admitted he was a sinner.
Moses never thought
of identifying himself with God.
Jesus is the only leader who dared say,
"Whoever has seen me
has seen the Father."
If Jesus was correct in what he said,
then his followers can claim access
to a unique knowledge of God.

What convinces me most
that Jesus was who he claimed to be?

If Jesus were to come today,
people would not crucify him.
They would ask him to dinner,
hear what he had to say,
and make fun of it.

THOMAS CARLYLE

WEEK 1: Learn of Me

_____ Day 5

Be glad about . . . [the] trials you suffer.
Their purpose
is to prove that your faith is genuine.
Even gold . . . is tested by fire;
and so your faith . . . must also be tested,
so that it may endure.

1 PETER 1:6-7

Newspaperman Hugh Kay
gave this advice to a young person
having faith problems:
"The darkness you are encountering
is in itself a rich experience.
If it be that you really want to meet
our Lord, then it is by moonlight that
you must seek him under an olive tree.
You will find him flat on the ground,
and you will have to lie down
on your face with him
if you are to catch his words."

To what gospel event is Kay referring,
and what is his point about having to
"lie down on your face with [Jesus]
if you are to catch his words"? What
faith problem bothers me sometimes?

How do I understand these words
of Kahlil Gibran:
"Doubt is a pain too lonely to know
that faith is its twin brother"?

WEEK 1: Learn of Me

Day 6 _____

The Father loves his Son
and has put everything in his power.
Whoever believes in the Son
has eternal life.

JOHN 3:35-36

Mike Moran was a navy helicopter pilot.
One day, while explaining his "chopper"
to his parents, he said,
"As complex as those machines are,
their whirling rotors are held in place
by one simple hexagonal nut."
Then, turning to his mother, he said,
"Guess what that nut is called, Mom."
She shrugged.
He smiled and said,
"It's called a 'Jesus Nut.'"

To what extent
does Jesus hold my life together?
What is one area of my life
that is still not under his control?
What is one step that I might take
to begin to let Jesus take control
of this area of my life?

Jesus is a path to the lost.
He is a loaf to the spiritually hungry.
He is an arm for the weak.
He is a companion to the lonely.
He is a beacon of hope for all.

[Jesus said,]
"My Father has given me all things.
No one knows . . . the Father
except the Son
and those to whom the Son chooses
to reveal him. . . .
Learn from me, because
I am gentle and humble in spirit."

MATTHEW 11:27, 29

The film *Lady Sings the Blues*
portrays the life of singer Billie Holiday.
Diana Ross, who plays Billie,
said that she spent months
preparing for her role.
She read miles of print about Billie's life
and listened to hours of Billie's songs.
"I was committed to doing a good job,"
she said. "I tried very hard
to know her as much as I could."

Diana's commitment
to making Billie live again on the screen
is a model for my commitment
to making Jesus live again in our world.
It invites me to ask, Am I as committed to
learning about Jesus
as Diana was to learning about Billie?

Be still, and know that I am God!

PSALM 46:10 (Grail)

WEEK 2:
Follow Me

WEEK 2: Follow Me

Day 1

The Word . . .
brought light to mankind.
The light shines in the darkness,
and the darkness has never put it out.

JOHN 1:4-5

An artist painted a picture
of a single person rowing a boat
across a vast sea at night.
Off in the distant sky is a single star.
The impression you get
as you look at the single person and
the single star is this:
If the person in that boat
ever loses sight of that star in the sky,
the person will be utterly lost.
What the painting says of that person
can be said of me:
If I ever lose sight of Jesus in my life,
I will be utterly lost.

What was the closest I ever came
to losing sight of Jesus in my life?
What kept Jesus in my sights then?

Jesus, be a bright star before me.
Be a silent wake behind me.
Be a rolling path beneath me.
Be a ray of light within me.
Be all these things—now and forever.

ANONYMOUS

WEEK 2: Follow Me

Day 2 _____

*[Barnabas and Saul
went to the city of Antioch.]
The two met with the people
of the church and taught a large group.
It was at Antioch that the believers
were first called Christians.*

ACTS 11:26

A woman was watching the distribution
of used clothing to street people.
Suddenly she found herself wondering,
"What would it be like
to walk about in another's clothes?
What would it be like
to walk about in another's shoes?"
Then it occurred to her:
That's what Christianity is all about.
It's about walking in another's shoes:
the shoes of Jesus.
It's about going where Jesus would go
and doing what Jesus would do.
It's about being Jesus in today's world.

How comfortable am I walking in Jesus'
shoes? Where do they "pinch" me most?

*Every character has an inward spring;
let Christ be that spring.
Every action has a keynote;
let Christ be that note.*

HENRY DRUMMOND

The LORD says, "The time is coming
when I will choose as king
a righteous descendant of David. . . .
When he is king,
the people of Judah will be safe. . . .
He will be called
'The LORD Our Salvation.' "

JEREMIAH 23:5-6

"To know Christ is not enough.
To be convinced
that he is the Savior of the world
is not enough.
To affirm your faith in him
as we do in the Apostles' Creed
is not enough.
You really don't actively believe
in Christ until you make
a commitment of your life to him
and receive him as your Savior."

BILLY GRAHAM

Concretely, what is meant by the phrase
"to receive Jesus as my Savior"?

Salvation is not something
that is done for you
but something that happens within you.
It is not the clearing of a court record,
but the transformation of a life attitude.

ALBERT W. PALMER

WEEK 2: Follow Me

Day 4 ───────────────

[Jesus said,]
"I am going to him who sent me. . . .
And now that I have told you,
your hearts are full of sadness.
But . . . it is better for you that I go away,
because if I do not go, the Helper
[Holy Spirit] will not come to you."

JOHN 16:5-7

A young Hindu and a young Christian
were taking the same seminar
on Jesus' Sermon on the Mount.
Very quickly, they became good friends.
One day the Hindu said to the Christian,
"I know how Jesus' Sermon on the Mount
affected Gandhi and influenced his life,
but I fear its teaching is too difficult
and too lofty for ordinary people."
Toward the end of the seminar,
the Hindu found the answer to his dilemma.
Jesus' teaching was indeed lofty,
but he had overlooked Jesus' promise
to send the Spirit—
who would empower us to live by it.

How frequently do I turn to the Spirit
for guidance and power?

Where the human spirit fails,
the Holy Spirit fills.

ANONYMOUS

WEEK 2: Follow Me

[Jesus said,]
"No one can be a slave of two masters;
he will hate one and love the other;
he will be loyal to one
and despise the other.
You cannot serve both God and money."

MATTHEW 6:24

A woman was about to take a shower.
She had one foot in the shower stall
and the other foot on the bathroom rug.
As she stood in this awkward position,
she thought to herself,
"This is a good picture of my life."
She wanted to commit her life to Jesus,
but she could never quite do it.
She kept one foot in and one foot out.
Now the time to decide had come.
She paused for a long time.
Then, taking a deep breath, she said aloud,
"I choose you, Jesus!"
With that, she stepped into the shower.
It was like being baptized.

What is one area
in my relationship with Jesus
where I am failing to be decisive,
keeping one foot in and one foot out?

Not to decide is to decide.
HARVEY COX

WEEK 2: Follow Me

Day 6 _____

[Jesus said the prophecies
about the Messiah applied to him.]
When the people
in the synagogue [at Nazareth]
heard this, they were filled with anger
[and rejected Jesus violently].

LUKE 4:28

Jesus' rejection
by the people of his hometown
previews what will take place often
in the days ahead: namely,
people will reject Jesus—even violently.
Today, people still reject Jesus and
his teaching.
When asked why he didn't follow Jesus,
a high school boy said bluntly,
"Because if I did,
many of my friends would reject me—
just as many of Jesus' friends
rejected him.
And I don't think I could take
that kind of rejection right now."

How much has peer pressure influenced
my following of Jesus in the past?
How much is it influencing it right now?

We forfeit three-fourths of ourselves
to be like other people.
ARTHUR SCHOPENHAUER

WEEK 2: Follow Me

——————————————————— Day 7

God is to be trusted,
the God who called you to have fellowship
with his Son Jesus Christ, our Lord.

1 CORINTHIANS 1:9

A poem compares following Jesus
to two people riding a tandem bicycle.
"At first, I sat in front; Jesus in the rear.
I couldn't see him, but I knew he was there.
I'd feel his help when the road got steep.
Then, one day, Jesus and I changed seats.
Suddenly everything went topsy-turvy.
When I was in control,
the ride was predictable—even boring.
But when Jesus took over, it got wild!
I could hardly hold on.
'This is madness!' I cried.
But Jesus just smiled—and said, 'Pedal!'
And so I learned to shut up and pedal—
and trust my bike companion.
Oh, there are still times
when I get scared and I'm ready to quit.
But Jesus turns, touches my hand, smiles,
and says, 'Pedal!' "

In what area, especially, do I find it hard
to trust my bike companion?

I may trust Jesus too little,
but I can never trust him too much.

ANONYMOUS

WEEK 3:
Your Light
Must Shine

WEEK 3: Your Light Must Shine

_____ Day 1

[Before ascending to heaven,
Jesus said to his disciples,]
"When the Holy Spirit comes upon you,
you will be filled with power,
and you will be witnesses for me . . .
to the ends of the earth."

ACTS 1:8

A high point in a relay race
is the passing of the baton
from one runner to another runner.
More races are won or lost
at this critical moment
than at any other moment in the race.
The event of Pentecost
might be compared to this key moment
The baton of God's kingdom
is passed by Jesus to his disciples.
They are to complete the work
he began while living among us.

What are some of my thoughts
as I imagine myself
taking the baton of God's kingdom
from the hand of Jesus?

God has created me
to do some definite service.
He has committed some work to me
which he has not committed to another.

JOHN HENRY NEWMAN

WEEK 3: Your Light Must Shine

Day 2 _____

[Jesus said to his disciples,
"When the Holy Spirit comes,
you will] speak about me,
because you have been with me
from the very beginning."

JOHN 15:27

Former Penn State football star
D. J. Dozier knelt and prayed
after he scored in the Fiesta Bowl.
His action sparked instant criticism.
Coming to his defense, R. D. Lashar,
an outstanding high school kicker, said,
"Before and after each place kick,
I kneel and pray.
The day someone tells me I can't pray
is the day I don't play!
It's a free country."
Sports fan Mark Roberts wrote,
"I find it refreshing to see someone
do something besides a silly dance . . .
and flaunting an oversized ego."

What is one way that I am giving
effective witness to Jesus
in my own personal work or activities?
Why do I feel this is effective?

Every believer in this world
must become a spark of light.

POPE JOHN XXIII

WEEK 3: Your Light Must Shine

The Spirit that God has given us
does not make us timid. . . .
Do not be ashamed, then,
of witnessing for our Lord.
                    2 TIMOTHY 1:7–8

A teacher had students take scissors
and cut a piece from a poster that was
covered over with paper.
"Take your piece home, but don't peek,"
she said. "Bring it back next Sunday."
The next Sunday, the students returned
to assemble the poster.
To their dismay, it had a big hole in it.
One little girl had forgotten her piece.
The teacher hugged the tearful girl
who forgot her piece, and said,
"Amy, I'm glad you forgot, because
it teaches better than I had anticipated
how important each of us is in God's plan.
Each of us is called
to witness to Jesus in some unique way;
and if we forget, God's plan loses
some of its beauty, just like this poster."

How might I better witness
to Jesus in my present work or activity?

Ten musical geniuses playing beautifully
cannot perform a symphony.
It takes a full *orchestra to perform it.*

WEEK 3: Your Light Must Shine

Day 4 ___

[After expelling an evil spirit
from a person, Jesus said,]
"Go back home to your family
and tell them
how much the Lord has done for you
and how kind he has been to you."
So the man left. . . .
And all who heard it were amazed.

MARK 5:19-20

Young Ruddell Norris was aware
that every Christian is called
by baptism and confirmation
to spread the good news of the Gospel.
His problem was that he was very shy.
Ruddell's solution was ingenious.
He spent a part of his allowance
on religious pamphlets
and placed them in hospital lobbies
and other appropriate places.
One day he overheard someone saying,
"My introduction to the church
came through a pamphlet
that I found in a hospital lobby."

What would tend to keep me from doing
the kind of thing Ruddell did?

It is not enough for me to love God,
if my neighbor does not love God.

SAINT VINCENT DE PAUL

WEEK 3: Your Light Must Shine

_____ Day 5

Whoever turns a sinner back
from his wrong way
will save the sinner's soul from death.
JAMES 5:19

Author Irene Champernowne
was walking along a beach one evening.
She came upon some small children
throwing stones at a crippled gull.
She stopped and said gently,
"That poor gull must be hurting a lot."
Then she explored with them
how they would feel
if they were hurt badly and
people tried to hurt them even more.
Half an hour later,
Irene returned from her walk
and was thrilled to see the children
feeding the gull and
building it a "house" for the night.

Can I recall one time in my life
when I protested in a constructive way
something I thought was wrong?

There may be times
when we are powerless
to prevent injustice,
but there must never be a time
when we fail to protest it.
ELIE WIESEL

WEEK 3: Your Light Must Shine

Day 6

*[Jesus was standing on the shore
watching Peter and some disciples
returning from a bad night of fishing.
Jesus said,]
"Throw your net out on the right side
of the boat, and you will catch some."
So they threw the net out
and could not pull it back in,
because they had caught so many fish.*

JOHN 21:6

*Children's Letters to God:
The New Collection,*
by Stuart Hample and Eric Marshall,
contains this delightful letter:
"God:
the bad people laghed at noah—
you make an ark on dry land you fool.
But he was smart he stuck with you.
that's what I would do.
Eddie"

Eddie was willing to stick with God,
even though people "laghed" at him.
How willing am I to stick with Jesus
even though people may "lagh" at me
for sticking with him?

*When the world seems at its worst,
Christians must be at their best.*

ANONYMOUS

WEEK 3: Your Light Must Shine

[Jesus said,]
"A man takes a mustard seed,
the smallest seed in the world,
and plants it in the ground. . . .
It grows up and
becomes the biggest of all plants.
It puts out such large branches
that the birds come and
make their nests in its shade."

MARK 4:31–32

Rosa Parks was a black seamstress.
One day in Alabama in 1955,
she was arrested, handcuffed, and jailed
for refusing to vacate a bus seat
reserved for whites.
That episode turned out to be the seed
out of which
grew the civil rights movement.
Ten years later, at the Freedom Festival,
Rosa was given the title "The First Lady
of the Civil Rights Movement."

Why do/don't I believe that one person
can make a difference in today's world?

Where is tomorrow born?
How does the future start?
On a winter's working day.
In a Negro woman's heart.

EVE MERRIAM

WEEK 4:
Pray

WEEK 4: Pray

<hr>

Day 1

*[Martha complained to Jesus because
Mary listened to him while she worked.
Jesus said,] "Martha, Martha! . . .
Mary has chosen the right thing,
and it will not be taken away from her."*

Luke 10:41–42

A young monk had questions
about the order's motto: "Pray and Work."
One day the abbot invited him
to row across the lake with him.
The abbot rowed first—but with one oar.
As a result, the boat went in circles.
The young monk said,
"Abbot, unless you row with both oars,
you won't get anywhere."
The abbot replied, "Ah! You're right, son!
The right oar is prayer; the left is work.
Unless you keep them in balance
and use them together,
you'll end up going in circles."

What kind of balance do I try to keep
between work and prayer? How can I
be sure I have the right balance?

*Each Christian needs at least
ten minutes of prayer a day,
except when we are busy.
Then we need at least twenty minutes.*

ANONYMOUS

WEEK 4: Pray

Day 2 _____

[One night Jacob camped under the stars.
In a dream, he saw God.]
Jacob woke up and said,
"The LORD is here!
He is in this place!"
[That dream changed his entire life.]

GENESIS 28:16

A high school student
wrote in a homework assignment:
"I was skiing all alone down a slope.
Suddenly I pulled up and stopped.
I still don't know why—
it was as if someone said, 'Stop, Chris!'
Everything was quiet and beautiful:
the clear blue sky above me,
the soft white snow below me,
green cedars on each side of me.
As I stood there,
a strange feeling came over me;
and a strange thought entered my mind:
'God is in this place!'
It was a moment I'll never forget."

What is the closest I ever came
to an experience such as that described
by the student and by Jacob?

I have always regarded nature
as the clothing of God.
ALAN HOVHANESS

[The crowds around Jesus got so big
that he] and his disciples
had no time to eat.
When his family heard about it,
they set out to take charge of him,
because people were saying,
"He's gone mad!"

MARK 3:20–21

J. D. Salinger wrote a story called "Teddy."
It's about a young person
who finds it next to impossible
to live a spiritual life in today's world.
Teddy says:
"I mean, it's very hard to meditate
and live a spiritual life in America.
People think you're a freak. . . .
My father thinks I'm a freak, in a way.
And my mother—
well, she doesn't think it's good for me
to think about God all the time."
Jesus had the same problem
with many of his friends and relatives.

How do people react to my efforts
to live a spiritual life in today's world?

Whenever you find yourself
on the side of the majority,
it is time to pause and reflect.
MARK TWAIN

WEEK 4: Pray

Day 4 _____

[Jesus prayed for his disciples, saying,]
"While I was with them,
I kept them safe by the power of . . .
the name you gave me. . . .
And now I am coming to you,
and I . . . ask you to keep them safe
from the Evil One."

John 17:12-13, 15

Praying is like plugging a lamp cord
into an electrical outlet.
Plugging the cord into the outlet
does not create the electrical power.
It simply makes contact with it.
It enables electrical power
to flow from the outlet,
through the cord, into the lamp.
It is the same with praying.
Praying does not create divine power.
It simply makes contact with it.
It enables divine power
to flow from God,
through us, into the lives of people.

What ought I to do if I don't seem to be
making contact with God in prayer?

Whoever has lost contact with God
lives on the same dead-end street
as the person who denies God.

MILTON MARCY

Day 5

A loyal friend is like a safe shelter;
find one, and you have found a treasure.
Nothing else is as valuable;
there is no way of putting a price on it.
                                    SIRACH 6:14-15

Robert Veninga describes
an Alcoholics Anonymous support group
in his book *A Gift of Hope*. He writes:
"The friendship among these seven men
is one of the strongest bonds of friendship
I have ever seen. . . .
Even when the executives
are traveling on business,
they make certain they fly home
for the Saturday night meeting.
It is just too precious to miss."

Can I recall a sacrifice I made to keep
from missing a meeting of my friends
in my prayer support group?

The glory of Friendship
is not the outstretched hand,
nor the kindly smile,
nor the joy of companionship;
it is the spiritual inspiration
that comes to one when he discovers
that someone else believes in him
and is willing to trust him.
                        RALPH WALDO EMERSON

WEEK 4: Pray

Day 6 _____

*[Jesus] threw himself face downward
on the ground, and prayed.*
MATTHEW 26:39

Three ministers were discussing
the best posture to use while praying.
The first said, "I've tried them all,
and kneeling is still the best."
The second said, "That may be true,
but most Eastern mystics recommend
sitting cross-legged on the floor."
The third said,
"I pray best with my eyes closed."
An electrician working nearby
overheard them and said,
"For what it's worth, fellas,
the best prayer I ever prayed
was when I was hanging by one leg
from a telephone pole in a thunderstorm."

Do I ever experiment with my posture
during prayer? For example, do I ever pray
the prayer before meditation out loud?
Do I ever pray with eyes lifted to heaven?

*Ahab folded his large brown hands
across his chest, uplifted closed eyes
and offered a prayer so devout
that he seemed kneeling and praying
at the bottom of the sea.*
HERMAN MELVILLE, *Moby Dick*

*[Jesus told a parable about a widow
who persevered in pleading for a long time
with a judge to help her get her rights.
He finally agreed to help, saying to himself,]*
"If I don't, she will . . . wear me out!"
*[Jesus ended the parable by saying
we should persevere in praying to God
the way the woman pleaded for help.]*

LUKE 18:3-5

Swiss psychiatrist Dr. Paul Tournier
dates his conversion to a day
when he chose to spend an hour praying.
It proved to be a dry, painful experience.
But when the hour was over,
something told him to pray a bit longer.
He did, and he ended up
experiencing God's presence in a way
that changed his life.
It frightened him to think
how close he had come to missing it.

What motivates me to persevere
in prayer, when it all seems impossible
and my heart refuses to cooperate?

*Pure love and prayer are learned
in the hour
when prayer has become impossible
and your heart has turned to stone.*
THOMAS MERTON

WEEK 5:
Do This in
Memory of Me

WEEK 5: Do This in Memory of Me

These people, says God,
honor me with their words,
but their heart
is really far away from me.
MATTHEW 15:8

A woman had a strange dream.
An angel took her to a church to worship.
The organist played,
the organ's keys went up and down,
but no music came from the organ.
The choir sang,
the singers' mouths opened and closed,
but no song came from their lips.
The congregation prayed,
their lips moved,
but no sound could be heard.
The woman turned to the angel and said,
"Why don't I hear anything?"
The angel said,
"There's nothing to hear."

How faithfully
do I try to worship my God and Savior
not just with my lips
but with my whole mind, heart, and soul?

We should give God
the same place in our hearts
that he holds in the universe.
ANONYMOUS

WEEK 5: Do This in Memory of Me

Day 2 _____

The church is Christ's body. . . .
[Jesus] is the head of his body, the church;
he is the source of the body's life. . . .
In union with Christ . . .
we are all joined to each other
as different parts of one body.
So we are to use our different gifts
in accordance with the grace
that God has given us.
  EPHESIANS 1:23, COLOSSIANS 1:18, ROMANS 12:5-6

A college girl said to her friend,
"Although I don't believe in the church,
I do believe in the Risen Jesus."
Her friend said, "How is that possible?
How can you separate the Risen Jesus
from his church?
Didn't the Holy Spirit unite the two
into one body on Pentecost?
Isn't trying to separate the two
like trying to separate
one's own body from one's own head?"

How would I answer the girl's friend?
How might I, also, be trying to separate
the head (Christ) from the body (church)?

If you don't have the church
for your mother,
you cannot have God for your Father.
  SAINT AUGUSTINE

WEEK 5: Do This in Memory of Me

_____ Day 3

[Jesus said,] "The Kingdom of heaven
is like this. Some fishermen
throw their net out in the lake
and catch all kinds of fish.
When the net is full, they pull it to shore
and sit down to divide the fish:
the good ones go into the buckets,
the worthless ones are thrown away.
It will be like this at the end of the age."
                              MATTHEW 13:47-49

Jesus compared the church to a net
that fishermen cast into the sea.
The net is open to all kinds of fish.
It's the same way with the church.
It's open to all kinds of people:
good people, selfish people,
thoughtless people.
When I find these people in the church,
I should not be surprised or disturbed.
Jesus said it would be this way.

How do I react to "imperfect" people
who seem to behave one way in church
and another way away from church?
How might I react more constructively?

If you find a perfect church,
by all means join it!
Then it will no longer be perfect.
                              BILLY GRAHAM

WEEK 5: Do This in Memory of Me

Day 1 _____

[Jesus said to his disciples,]
"You can do nothing without me.
Whoever does not remain in me
is thrown out like a branch and dries up."

JOHN 15:5-6

An old Jewish story concerns a woman
who stopped going to the synagogue.
One day the rabbi went to her house
and asked to come in
and sit with her by the fireplace.
For a long time, neither spoke.
Then the rabbi picked up some tongs,
took a glowing coal from the fireplace,
and set it on the hearth.
As the two watched,
the coal slowly lost its glow and died.
A few minutes later,
the old woman said, "I understand.
I'll come back to the synagogue."

Is there anyone who has been cut off
from Jesus whom I might help,
as the rabbi helped the old woman?
What might I do to help him or her?

He drew a circle that shut me out—
Heretic, rebel, a thing to flout.
But love and I had the wit to win.
We drew a circle that took him in.

EDWIN MARKHAM, "Outwitted"

WEEK 5: Do This in Memory of Me

*Many of his followers heard this
[Jesus' teaching about eating
his body and blood] and said,
"This teaching is too hard . . ."
and would not go with him any more.*
JOHN 6:60, 66

Many of us have shared the Lord's Supper
since childhood.
But if we are honest, we must admit
that this has not brought us
as close to Jesus and one another
as we had hoped that it would. Why?
Perhaps it's because we tend to view
the Lord's Supper only as a meal:
a time of receiving.
We forget it is also a sacrifice:
a time of giving and forgiving.
We forget that unless we walk with Jesus
in the shadows of Good Friday (sacrifice),
we won't be able to walk with him
in the blazing sunlight of Easter (meal).

How faithfully am I walking with Jesus
in the shadows of Good Friday?
How might I walk even more faithfully?

*The effect of our receiving
the body and blood of Christ
is to change us into what we receive.*
POPE SAINT LEO THE GREAT

WEEK 5: Do This in Memory of Me

Day 6 _____

[Jesus] taught in the synagogue, and
those who heard him were amazed. . . .
"Isn't he the carpenter's son? . . .
Where did he get all this?"
And so they rejected him.

MATTHEW 13:53-57

A teacher asked her students,
"Who is the most important person
present during the homily at Mass?"
Most of the students responded,
"The homilist!" But one girl said,
"Three persons are present,
and they are all equally important:
the homilist, me, and the Holy Spirit.
The homilist is very important.
But my openness to his words
is equally important.
If I'm not open to his words,
there's little the homilist can do or say.
On the other hand, if I'm open to them,
the Holy Spirit can use them
to speak to me,
even if the homilist is dull or boring."

Can I think of an example to illustrate
the girl's final point?
What is one homily that touched me?

Speak, LORD, your servant is listening.

1 SAMUEL 3:10

WEEK 5: Do This in Memory of Me

Where two or three
come together in my name,
I am there with them.
MATTHEW 18:20

The Kwa Noi prison camp in Thailand
was a living hell
for American and British soldiers
in World War II.
Then one day a couple of prisoners
organized faith-sharing groups.
The camp situation changed dramatically.
A prisoner recalls the change this way.
He was hobbling back to his shack
one night after a late Bible session.
Suddenly he heard a group of men singing
"Jerusalem the Golden." He wrote later:
"The words of that grand old hymn . . .
made the darkness seem friendly. . . .
The difference between this joyful sound
and the joyless stillness of months past
was the difference between life and death."
It is this kind of difference Jesus made—
and still makes—in our world.

What is one way
Jesus has made a difference in my life?

I have a great need for Christ;
I have a great Christ for my need.
CHARLES SPURGEON

WEEK 6:
Wash One
Another's Feet

WEEK 6: Wash One Another's Feet

[Before ascending to the Father,
Jesus said to his disciples,]
"Go . . . to all peoples everywhere
and make them my disciples. . . .
And I will be with you always."

MATTHEW 28:18-20

A woman saw a little girl on the street.
The child was poorly dressed,
ill-nourished, and
playing in the gutter with filthy trash.
The woman became angry
and said to God,
"Why do you let a thing like that
happen in the world you created?
Why don't you do something about it?"
God replied, "I did do something about it;
I created you."

That story invites me to ask, How might
I respond better to Jesus' invitation
to help him transform our world into
the kind of place God created it to be?

The Ascension of Christ
is his liberation from all restrictions
of time and space.
It does not represent his removal
from earth, but his constant presence
everywhere on earth.

WILLIAM TEMPLE

WEEK 6: Wash One Another's Feet

Day 2 _____

[Jesus washed his disciples' feet,
saying to them,] "Wash one another's feet."
JOHN 13:14

Doing volunteer work
at a home for runaways, Anne Donohue
became angry with God, saying,
"Why don't you show them the love
their parents didn't show them? Why?"
Then it dawned on her!
God wants to do this for them.
But God can do it only through us.
We are God's voice;
we are God's hands; we are God's heart.

What do I find hardest about letting God
speak through *my* voice,
lift burdens with *my* hands,
love the unfortunate with *my* heart?

We are on our way to Venus,
but we still haven't learned
to live together on earth.
We have increased our life span,
but we exterminate our brothers and
sisters, six million at a whack.
We have the power
to destroy ourselves and our planet.
Depend upon it, we will—
if we ever stop loving.

HARPER LEE (adapted)

WEEK 6: Wash One Another's Feet

[Jesus said, "The King will reply,]
'I tell you, whenever you did this
for one of the least important
of these brothers [or sisters]
of mine, . . . you did it for me!' "
MATTHEW 25:40

Sandra Hook is a Canadian teacher.
One summer
she was doing volunteer work
with Mother Teresa among India's poor.
The day came
when she was asked to bathe a woman
who was covered with sores.
She shuddered at the thought of it.
Then she remembered
what Mother Teresa had said:
"When you touch the poor,
touch them the way you would touch
Jesus himself."
At that moment Sandra saw the woman
through the eyes of faith
and had no difficulty bathing her.

What do I understand by the expression
"through the eyes of faith"?
How can I learn to see with these eyes?

Only when we learn to see the invisible
will we learn to do the impossible.
FRANK GAINES (slightly adapted)

WEEK 6: Wash One Another's Feet

Day 4 _____

[Jesus said,] "And now I give you
a new commandment: love one another.
As I have loved you,
so you must love one another.
If you have love for one another,
then everyone will know
that you are my disciples."

JOHN 13:34–35

Federico Fellini's film *La Strada*
opened in 1954 and became a classic.
In one unforgettable scene,
a clown is talking to a young lady.
She has grown weary of trying to love
unlovable and unloving people, and
she wants nothing more to do with them.
As the conversation ends
and the young lady turns to leave,
the clown says to her,
"But if you don't love these people,
who will love them?"

What answer would I give to the clown?
Can I recall a time when I helped someone
whom I did not find lovable?
What motivated me to do it?

To love the world is no big chore.
It's that miserable person next door
who is the problem.

ANONYMOUS

WEEK 6: Wash One Another's Feet

[Paul writes:]
Be an example for the believers
in your speech, your conduct,
your love, faith, and purity.

1 TIMOTHY 4:12

Dr. Lloyd Judd contracted cancer.
Before he died,
he made a series of tapes
to be played
when his children were old enough
to appreciate them.
On one of the tapes he said to them,
"Are you willing to get out of a warm bed
in the middle of the night,
when you desperately need rest,
and drive twenty miles—
knowing you will not be paid—
to see someone
you know can wait until morning? . . .
If you can answer yes to this,
I feel you are qualified
to start the study of medicine."

How would I answer Dr. Judd's question?
How would I explain my answer
to Jesus or the Holy Spirit?

We stand tallest
when we bend over to help the fallen.

ANONYMOUS

WEEK 6: Wash One Another's Feet

Day 6 _____

Jerusalem . . .
has not listened to the LORD. . . .
It has not put its trust in the LORD
or asked for his help.

ZEPHANIAH 3:1–2

George Burns played the part of God
in a movie called *Oh, God!*
In the same movie, John Denver
played a supermarket employee.
One day God gave the employee
a message for the world.
Getting people to believe the message
turned out to be next to impossible.
The employee was ridiculed
and called a "religious nut."
He grew angry
and complained bitterly to God.
The employee's reaction
was very much like Jerusalem's reaction
in today's reading.
Instead of trusting and asking for help,
he simply got angry and complained.

How do I react when I run into problems
in my service of God?

Do not be afraid or discouraged,
for I, the LORD your God,
am with you wherever you go.

JOSHUA 1:9

WEEK 6: Wash One Another's Feet

[The LORD said to Israel,]
"What I want from you is plain and clear:
I want your constant love."

HOSEA 6:5-6

Film director Jean-Jacques Arnaud
said the movie *Quest for Fire*
fulfilled a lifelong dream.
It celebrated the discovery of fire,
which took place 80,000 years ago—
a discovery that saved the human race
from extinction.
Today, many people fear that we are,
once again, on the brink of extinction.
Only one thing can save us:
the rediscovery of love—the kind of love
that God talks about in today's reading.
People wonder,
"Will someone, 80,000 years from now,
make a movie
to celebrate the rediscovery of love
that saved the human race from
extinction in the year 2000?"

What is one concrete step
that I can take, right now in my life,
to contribute to the rediscovery of love?

No one needs love more
than someone who doesn't deserve it.

ANONYMOUS

WEEK 7:
Bear Much Fruit

WEEK 7: Bear Much Fruit

[Jesus prayed for his disciples, saying,]
"Holy Father! . . .
I gave them your message. . . .
I sent them into the world,
just as you sent me into the world.
And for their sake I dedicate myself
to you, in order that they, too,
may be truly dedicated to you."

JOHN 17:11, 14, 17-18

Legend says that when Jesus returned
to heaven, the angel Gabriel asked him
if all people knew of his love for them.
"Oh, no!" said Jesus. "Only a handful do."
Gabriel was shocked and asked,
"How will the rest learn?"
Jesus said, "The handful will tell them."
"But," said Gabriel,
"what if they let you down?
What if they meet opposition?
What if they become discouraged?
Don't you have a backup plan?"
"No," said Jesus, "I'm counting on them
not to let me down."

What convinces me that
Jesus' followers won't let him down?

I used to ask God to help me.
Then I asked if I might help him.

HUDSON TAYLOR

WEEK 7: Bear Much Fruit

Day 2 _____

[Paul writes:]
God gave me the privilege of
being an apostle for the sake of Christ,
in order to lead people of all nations
to believe.

ROMANS 1:5

There's a humorous story
about a woman who saw a sparrow
lying on its back,
holding its legs toward the sky.
The woman asked the tiny sparrow,
"Why are you lying like that?"
The sparrow replied,
"We're told the sky is going to fall today."
The woman laughed uproariously
and said to the sparrow,
"Do you think
your toothpick legs will hold up the sky?"
"No," said the sparrow,
"but I must do what I can."

When it comes to working for the spread
of God's kingdom on earth,
to what extent do I live out the philosophy
of the sparrow in the story?

The only failure
that is truly tragic is not
to try and fail, but to fail to try.
ANONYMOUS

WEEK 7: Bear Much Fruit

[One day Jesus asked his disciples
for their loaves to help feed a crowd.
Jesus took them,]
gave thanks to God,
broke them, and gave them . . .
to the people.
They all ate and had enough.

MATTHEW 15:35-37

Mother Teresa
felt called by Jesus to help the poor,
especially the children in India's slums.
She began by using all the money she had
to buy a small dirt-floor shack.
Today that shack has multiplied itself
into over 100 schools for children
and over 150 homes for dying people.
Mother Teresa
gave her "loaves and fishes" to Jesus,
and he multiplied them
beyond her wildest dreams.

What "loaves and fishes" can I give
to Jesus to be multiplied by him?

Yours are the only hands
with which he can do his work. . . .
Yours are the only eyes
through which his compassion
can shine upon a troubled world.

SAINT TERESA OF AVILA

WEEK 7: Bear Much Fruit

Day 4 _____

*[Some magi from the East] saw his star
when it came up in the east.*

MATTHEW 2:2

Henry Van Dyke wrote a story about
an imaginary fourth wise man, Artaban.
He was to go with the other three
to search for the newborn king.
Artaban had a pouch of precious gems
as a gift for the baby king.
On his way to join the other three,
he stopped to help a needy person.
The delay was just enough
to cause him to miss the other magi.
He never did catch them; he kept helping
people and giving away all his gems.
Artaban ended up as a beggar
in a faraway city called Jerusalem.
One day he saw a criminal
being marched off to be executed.
He felt close to this man and was sad
that he couldn't help him.
As the man drew near, he turned
to Artaban and said, "Be not sad.
You've been helping me all your life."

How do I imagine Artaban felt
when Jesus said this to him?

When you helped the needy, you helped me.

MATTHEW 25:40 (paraphrased)

WEEK 7: Bear Much Fruit

_____ Day 5

*[Jeremiah confronted the people about
their sins, as the LORD commanded.
They reacted by mistreating him.
Jeremiah said,]
They grabbed me and shouted,
"You ought to be killed for this!"*

JEREMIAH 26:8

Professor Samuel Langley achieved
the first unmanned air flight in 1896.
Just before the Wright brothers achieved
the first manned flight seven years later,
the *New York Times* wrote:
"We hope Professor Langley will not put
his substantial greatness as a scientist
in further peril
by continuing to waste his time
and the money involved
in further airship experiments. . . .
For students and investigators
of the Langley type,
there are more useful employments."

Can I recall being mistreated or ridiculed
for doing what I thought was right?
How did this mistreatment and ridicule
affect me?

*[The apostles] were happy . . .
to suffer disgrace for the sake of Jesus.*

ACTS 5:41

WEEK 7: Bear Much Fruit

Day 6 _____   _____

*[The disciples were crossing the lake
at night when a storm blew up.
Jesus came to them across the water.
They were utterly terrified.]* "Don't be
afraid," Jesus told them, "it is I!"

JOHN 6:20

A woman had been meditating and
meeting regularly for several months.
One morning she shared the following
with her group.
"I've gotten so much from this," she began,
"but lately I've begun to fear
where Jesus might be leading me.
Is he going to ask of me
some great sacrifice?"
An older woman, who had been listening
intently, said, "Susan, don't be afraid!
I once felt the same way you now feel.
And Jesus was, indeed, leading me—
just as he is leading you also.
As a result, I'm doing things now
I never dreamed I'd ever do.
But it's filled me with a joy and a peace
that I never dreamed existed."

Do I ever feel Jesus is leading me?
Do I ever fear where he is leading me?

What can I fear when I am with God?
BROTHER LAWRENCE

WEEK 7: Bear Much Fruit

My ambition has always been
to proclaim the Good News in places
where Christ has not been heard of.
ROMANS 15:20

Television's Phil Donahue
says that commitment is made up
of three stages.
First, there is the *fun* stage.
That's when I say, "I love doing this.
Why didn't I get involved sooner?"
Then there's the *intolerant* stage.
That's when I say,
"Anyone who's not involved
isn't really Christian!"
Finally, there's the *reality* stage.
That's when I realize my involvement
will probably make only a slight dent
in the war against evil.
It's at that stage that saints are made.

At what stage am I?
What motivates me to stay involved?

The happiest people in the world
are those
who have found the life task
to which they have been called. . . .
[And the unhappiest] are those
who have not even begun to search.
ROBERT C. LESLIE

Weekly Meeting Format

CALL TO PRAYER

> *The leader begins each weekly meeting*
> *by having someone light a candle*
> *and then three people pray the following:*

FIRST READER:
Jesus said,
"I am the light of the world. . . .
Whoever follows me
will have the light of life
and will never walk in darkness."

JOHN 8:12

SECOND READER:
Lord Jesus, you also said
that where two or three
come together in your name,
you are there with them.
The light of this candle
symbolizes your presence among us.

THIRD READER:
And, Lord Jesus,
where you are,
there, too,
are the Father and the Holy Spirit.
So we begin our meeting
in the presence and the name
of the Father,
the Son,
and the Holy Spirit.